# TOP 100
# High-Frequency Words

Learn the **Most Common High-Impact Words** in English!

created by
**Wiley Blevins**

# Welcome to High-Q!

**Wiley Blevins**
*Literacy Expert*

**Dear Families and Educators,**

High-frequency words are the most common words in English. These words are essential for children to learn early because they have high impact on a child's reading and writing growth. These are the words children are most likely to encounter in books they read or need to use in their writing.

The goal for all high-frequency words (as well as many other words) is that they become sight words. A sight word is any word—high-frequency or not—that a reader can identify automatically.

**What makes high-frequency words sometimes difficult?**
Some of these words are what we call "irregular." That is, they do not follow the most common sound-spelling (phonics skills) taught in the early years of a child's education. As such, the spellings of these words need to be learned by memory.

That doesn't mean a child must memorize the word as a whole chunk. In fact, to commit a word to memory, through a process called orthographic mapping, a reader must attend to the individual sounds and spellings in the word.

**Use the Read/Spell/Write routine on page 4–5** to help accelerate children's learning of these words by focusing on how the words are stored in memory.

Happy learning!

Wiley Blevins,
*Literacy Expert*

2

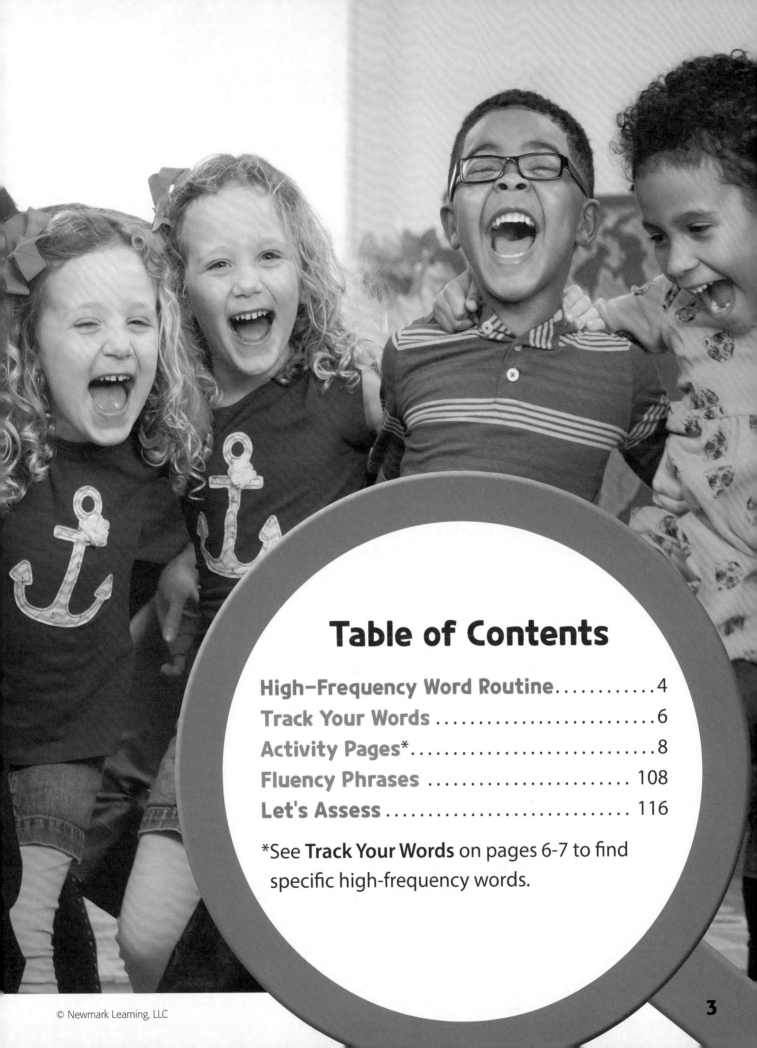

# Table of Contents

*See **Track Your Words** on pages 6-7 to find specific high-frequency words.

# High-Frequency Word Routine

Use the following routine to introduce the high-frequency words.

## Read

Point to the word and read it aloud. Then have children chorally read it. To build orthographic mapping of the word into memory for automatic retrieval, do the following:

Guide children to orally segment the word. Say:
*How many sounds do you hear in _____?*
*Let's tap the sounds as we say them.*

### Extra Support

For children who need extra support, give them Sound Boxes and counters. Guide them to stretch the sounds in the word as they move one counter onto each box for each sound they say. They can also point to the Sound Boxes on the activity page as they stretch and say the sounds in the word. Note that the gray boxes represent silent letters and do not count in the total number of sounds in the word.

Discuss known sound-spellings in the word. Then highlight any part that is irregular or unknown at that point in the child's instruction. This is the part of the word they will need to remember.

| Sample 1 | Sample 2 | Sample 3 |
|---|---|---|
| *What sounds do you hear in **of**? (/u/ /v/) What letters do you see? (o-f) The word **of** doesn't follow the rules. This is a word we have to pay extra attention to in order to remember its spelling.* | *What sounds do you hear in **said**? (/s/ /e/ /d/) What letters do you see? (s-a-i-d) Notice that the **ai** spelling stands for the middle /e/ sound instead of the letter **e**. That's the part of the word that we need to remember.* | *What sounds do you hear in **come**? (/k/ /u/ /m/) What letters do you see? (c-o-m-e) The **o_e** spelling stands for the /u/ sound, just like in the word **some**.* |

## Spell

Have children chorally spell the word as you point to each letter.

### Extra Support

For children still learning letter names, do an echo spell first.

## Write

Have children write the word as they spell it aloud. Note that on the activity page, any irregular or more difficult spellings are written in the heart shapes so you can draw children's attention to the parts they need to remember "by heart."

### Extra Support

For children who need more support, have them write the word on one side of a note card. On the back, co-construct a simple sentence with them. Write the sentences for them to copy on the back of the note card. Have children use the note cards as flashcards, reading the words in isolation and in context multiple times throughout the week and upcoming weeks.

# Track Your Words

Look for a word you want to learn.
Turn to that page.

Color each box after you finish the page.

| old | p. 60 | said | p. 73 | this | p. 86 | | |
| on | p. 61 | see | p. 74 | three | p. 87 | | |
| one | p. 62 | she | p. 75 | to | p. 88 | | |
| or | p. 63 | some | p. 76 | two | p. 89 | | |
| other | p. 64 | ten | p. 77 | up | p. 90 | which | p. 99 |
| our | p. 65 | that | p. 78 | use | p. 91 | who | p. 100 |
| out | p. 66 | the | p. 79 | want | p. 92 | why | p. 101 |
| people | p. 67 | their | p. 80 | was | p. 93 | will | p. 102 |
| play | p. 68 | them | p. 81 | we | p. 94 | with | p. 103 |
| pull | p. 69 | then | p. 82 | were | p. 95 | write | p. 104 |
| put | p. 70 | there | p. 83 | what | p. 96 | yes | p. 105 |
| read | p. 71 | these | p. 84 | when | p. 97 | you | p. 106 |
| run | p. 72 | they | p. 85 | where | p. 98 | your | p. 107 |

Name _____

## Read

**A. Read the word.**

a

How many sounds do you hear?
Point to the box as you say the sound.

a

## Spell

**B. Spell the word out loud as you write it.**

_____

## Write

**C. Write the word two times.**

_____    _____

**D. Write a sentence for the word.**

I am a _____

_____

_____ .

Name _____

## Read

**A.** **Read the word.**

all

How many sounds do you hear?

Point to each box as you say the sounds.

| a | ll |

## Spell

**B.** **Spell the word out loud as you write it.**

## Write

**C.** **Write the word two times.**

_____    _____

**D.** **Write a sentence for the word.**

All my friends _____

_____

_____ .

Name _____

## Read

**A. Read the word.**

am

How many sounds do you hear?

Point to each box as you say the sounds.

a    m

## Spell

**B. Spell the word out loud as you write it.**

_____   _____

## Write

**C. Write the word two times.**

_____    _____
- - - - - - - - - - - - - - - -    - - - - - - - - - - - - - - - -
_____    _____

**D. Write a sentence for the word.**

I am _____

_____

_____ .

# and

Name _____

## Read

**A. Read the word.**

and

How many sounds do you hear?
Point to each box as you say the sounds.

a    n    d

## Spell

**B. Spell the word out loud as you write it.**

_____ _____ _____

## Write

**C. Write the word two times.**

_____   _____

**D. Write a sentence for the word.**

I like _____ and

_____ .

# are

## Read

**A. Read the word.**

are

How many sounds do you hear? Point to each box as you say the sounds. The gray box is silent.

a    r    e

## Spell

**B. Spell the word out loud as you write it.**

_____  _____ ♡

## Write

**C. Write the word two times.**

_____  _____

**D. Write a sentence for the word.**

We are _____

_____ .

12

# at

## Read

**A. Read the word.**

at

How many sounds do you hear?

Point to each box as you say the sounds.

a      t

## Spell

**B. Spell the word out loud as you write it.**

_____   _____

## Write

**C. Write the word two times.**

_____   _____

**D. Write a sentence for the word.**

I am at the _____

_____ .

# be

## Read

**A. Read the word.**

be

How many sounds do you hear?

Point to each box as you say the sounds.

b    e

## Spell

**B. Spell the word out loud as you write it.**

_____ _____

## Write

**C. Write the word two times.**

**D. Write a sentence for the word.**

I will be _____

_____

_____ .

# big

## Read

**A. Read the word.**

big

How many sounds do you hear?

Point to each box as you say the sounds.

b     i     g

## Spell

**B. Spell the word out loud as you write it.**

_____  _____  _____

## Write

**C. Write the word two times.**

_____  _____

**D. Write a sentence for the word.**

The _____

_____

_____ is big.

# can

Name _____

## Read

**A. Read the word.**

| can | How many sounds do you hear?<br>Point to each box as you say the sounds. |

c    a    n

## Spell

**B. Spell the word out loud as you write it.**

_____  _____  _____

## Write

**C. Write the word two times.**

_____  _____

**D. Write a sentence for the word.**

I can _____

_____

_____ !

# come

## Read

**A. Read the word.**

come

How many sounds do you hear? Point to each box as you say the sounds. The gray box is silent.

c     o     m     e

## Spell

**B. Spell the word out loud as you write it.**

## Write

**C. Write the word two times.**

_____     _____

**D. Write a sentence for the word.**

_____

Come with me to _____

_____

_____ .

# could

## Read

**A. Read the word.**

could

How many sounds do you hear? Point to each box as you say the sounds. The gray box is silent.

| c | ou | l | d |

## Spell

**B. Spell the word out loud as you write it.**

## Write

**C. Write the word two times.**

_____    _____

_____    _____

**D. Write a sentence for the word.**

I wish I could _____

_____ !

# did

Name _____

## Read

**A.  Read the word.**

did

How many sounds do you hear?

Point to each box as you say the sounds.

| d | i | d |
|---|---|---|

## Spell

**B.  Spell the word out loud as you write it.**

_____  _____  _____

## Write

**C.  Write the word two times.**

_____    _____

**D.  Write a sentence for the word.**

I did not  _____

_____

_____ !

# different

## Read

**A. Read the word.**

 different

How many sounds do you hear? Point to each box as you say the sounds. The gray box is silent.

| d | i | ff | e | r | e | n | t |
|---|---|----|---|---|---|---|---|

## Spell

**B. Spell the word out loud as you write it.**

____ ____  ____ ____ ____ ____

## Write

**C. Write the word two times.**

_____        _____

**D. Write a sentence for the word.**

A _____ is different from a

_____ .

# do

## Read

**A. Read the word.**

do

How many sounds do you hear?

Point to each box as you say the sounds.

d     o

## Spell

**B. Spell the word out loud as you write it.**

## Write

**C. Write the word two times.**

_____     _____

**D. Write a sentence for the word.**

Do you _____

_____ ?

# down

## Read

**A. Read the word.**

down

How many sounds do you hear?

Point to each box as you say the sounds.

d | ow | n

## Spell

**B. Spell the word out loud as you write it.**

_____  _____  _____  _____

## Write

**C. Write the word two times.**

_____  _____

**D. Write a sentence for the word.**

fell down.

22

# eat

## Read

**A. Read the word.**

eat

How many sounds do you hear?

Point to each box as you say the sounds.

| ea | t |

## Spell

**B. Spell the word out loud as you write it.**

_____  _____  _____

## Write

**C. Write the word two times.**

_____  _____

**D. Write a sentence for the word.**

I like to eat _____

_____

_____ .

# eight

## Read

**A.  Read the word.**

eight

How many sounds do you hear?

Point to each box as you say the sounds.

eigh   t

## Spell

**B.  Spell the word out loud as you write it.**

♡ ♡ ♡ ♡ ____

## Write

**C.  Write the word two times.**

_____    _____

**D.  Write a sentence for the word.**

I have eight

_____

_____ .

24

# for

## Read

**A.** Read the word.

for

How many sounds do you hear?

Point to each box as you say the sounds.

| f | o | r |
|---|---|---|

## Spell

**B.** Spell the word out loud as you write it.

_____  _____  _____

## Write

**C.** Write the word two times.

_____  _____
_____  _____

**D.** Write a sentence for the word.

I need _____ for

_____ .

# four

## Read

**A. Read the word.**

four

How many sounds do you hear?

Point to each box as you say the sounds.

| f | ou | r |
|---|----|---|

## Spell

**B. Spell the word out loud as you write it.**

## Write

**C. Write the word two times.**

_____  _____

**D. Write a sentence for the word.**

A _____

_____ has four legs.

# from

## Read

**A.** **Read the word.**

from

How many sounds do you hear?

Point to each box as you say the sounds.

| f | r | o | m |

## Spell

**B.** **Spell the word out loud as you write it.**

_____ _____ ♡ _____

## Write

**C.** **Write the word two times.**

_____    _____

**D.** **Write a sentence for the word.**

I am from _____

_____ .

# give

## Read

**A. Read the word.**

give

How many sounds do you hear? Point to each box as you say the sounds. The gray box is silent.

g    i    v    e

## Spell

**B. Spell the word out loud as you write it.**

____ ____ ____

## Write

**C. Write the word two times.**

_____    _____

**D. Write a sentence for the word.**

Please give me _____

_____ .

Name _____

## Read

**A.   Read the word.**

go

How many sounds do you hear?

Point to each box as you say the sounds.

| g | o |
|---|---|

## Spell

**B.   Spell the word out loud as you write it.**

_____   _____

## Write

**C.   Write the word two times.**

_____     _____

**D.   Write a sentence for the word.**

I will go to _____

_____ .

# good

Name _____

**A.   Read the word.**

good

How many sounds do you hear?

Point to each box as you say the sounds.

| g | oo | d |

**Spell**

**B.   Spell the word out loud as you write it.**

_____   _____   _____   _____

**Write**

**C.   Write the word two times.**

_____   _____

**D.   Write a sentence for the word.**

_____

_____

_____

_____ are good to eat.

**30**

# had

## Read

**A. Read the word.**

had

How many sounds do you hear?

Point to each box as you say the sounds.

h   a   d

## Spell

**B. Spell the word out loud as you write it.**

_____   _____   _____

## Write

**C. Write the word two times.**

_____   _____

**D. Write a sentence for the word.**

I had to _____

_____ .

# has

## Read

**A.   Read the word.**

has

How many sounds do you hear?

Point to each box as you say the sounds.

h      a      s

## Spell

**B.   Spell the word out loud as you write it.**

_____   _____

## Write

**C.   Write the word two times.**

_____    _____

**D.   Write a sentence for the word.**

He has  _____

_____

_____ .

# have

## Read

**A.  Read the word.**

have

How many sounds do you hear? Point to each box as you say the sounds. The gray box is silent.

h   a   v   e

## Spell

**B.  Spell the word out loud as you write it.**

_____  _____  _____

## Write

**C.  Write the word two times.**

_____  _____

**D.  Write a sentence for the word.**

I have _____

_____ .

Name _____

## Read

**A.** **Read the word.**

he

How many sounds do you hear?

Point to each box as you say the sounds.

h    e

## Spell

**B.** **Spell the word out loud as you write it.**

_____    _____

## Write

**C.** **Write the word two times.**

_____    _____

**D.** **Write a sentence for the word.**

He can _____

_____ .

# her

## Read

**A. Read the word.**

her

How many sounds do you hear?

Point to each box as you say the sounds.

| h | e | r |

## Spell

**B. Spell the word out loud as you write it.**

_____  _____  _____

## Write

**C. Write the word two times.**

_____  _____

**D. Write a sentence for the word.**

Her _____ is

_____ .

# here

## Read

**A.  Read the word.**

here

How many sounds do you hear? Point to each box as you say the sounds. The gray box is silent.

| h | e | r | e |
|---|---|---|---|

## Spell

**B.  Spell the word out loud as you write it.**

_____ _____ _____ ♡

## Write

**C.  Write the word two times.**

_____    _____

**D.  Write a sentence for the word.**

Here is my _____

_____ .

# him

## Read

**A.** Read the word.

him

How many sounds do you hear?

Point to each box as you say the sounds.

| h | i | m |

## Spell

**B.** Spell the word out loud as you write it.

_____  _____  _____

## Write

**C.** Write the word two times.

_____    _____

**D.** Write a sentence for the word.

Tell him to _____

_____ .

# his

Name _____

**A.  Read the word.**

his

How many sounds do you hear?

Point to each box as you say the sounds.

h     i     s

## Spell

**B.  Spell the word out loud as you write it.**

_____  _____

## Write

**C.  Write the word two times.**

_____    _____

**D.  Write a sentence for the word.**

His dog is _____

_____

_____ .

# how

## Read

**A. Read the word.**

how

How many sounds do you hear?

Point to each box as you say the sounds.

h     ow

## Spell

**B. Spell the word out loud as you write it.**

_____   _____   _____

## Write

**C. Write the word two times.**

_____   _____

**D. Write a sentence for the word.**

How can I _____

_____ ?

Name _____

## Read

**A.   Read the word.**

I

How many sounds do you hear?

Point to the box as you say the sound.

I

## Spell

**B.   Spell the word out loud as you write it.**

_____

## Write

**C.   Write the word two times.**

_____        _____
- - - - - - - - -        - - - - - - - - -

**D.   Write a sentence for the word.**

I can _____

_____

_____ !

Name _____

## Read

**A. Read the word.**

in

How many sounds do you hear?

Point to each box as you say the sounds.

i     n

## Spell

**B. Spell the word out loud as you write it.**

_____    _____

## Write

**C. Write the word two times.**

_____    _____

**D. Write a sentence for the word.**

It is in _____

_____

_____ .

Name _____

## Read

**A.** **Read the word.**

How many sounds do you hear?

Point to each box as you say the sounds.

## Spell

**B.** **Spell the word out loud as you write it.**

## Write

**C.** **Write the word two times.**

_____     _____
- - - - - - - - - - - - - - -     - - - - - - - - - - - - - - -

**D.** **Write a sentence for the word.**

The cat is _____

_____

_____ .

Name _____

## Read

**A. Read the word.**

it

How many sounds do you hear?

Point to each box as you say the sounds.

i    t

## Spell

**B. Spell the word out loud as you write it.**

_____    _____

## Write

**C. Write the word two times.**

_____    _____

**D. Write a sentence for the word.**

Is it a _____

_____ ?

# jump

Name _____

## Read

**A.  Read the word.**

jump

How many sounds do you hear?

Point to each box as you say the sounds.

j    u    m    p

## Spell

**B.  Spell the word out loud as you write it.**

_____  _____  _____  _____

## Write

**C.  Write the word two times.**

_____    _____

**D.  Write a sentence for the word.**

Jump on the _____

_____

_____ .

# know

## Read

**A. Read the word.**

know

How many sounds do you hear? Point to each box as you say the sounds. The gray box is silent.

k    n    ow

## Spell

**B. Spell the word out loud as you write it.**

_____ _____ _____

## Write

**C. Write the word two times.**

_____    _____

**D. Write a sentence for the word.**

I know how to _____

_____ .

# let

## Read

**A. Read the word.**

let

How many sounds do you hear?

Point to each box as you say the sounds.

| l | e | t |

## Spell

**B. Spell the word out loud as you write it.**

_____   _____   _____

## Write

**C. Write the word two times.**

_____   _____
- - - - - - - - - - - - - - - -   - - - - - - - - - - - - - - - -

**D. Write a sentence for the word.**

Let me _____

_____ .

# like

Name _____

## Read

**A. Read the word.**

like

How many sounds do you hear? Point to each box as you say the sounds. The gray box is silent.

| l | i | k | e |

## Spell

**B. Spell the word out loud as you write it.**

_____ _____ _____ ♡

## Write

**C. Write the word two times.**

_____     _____

**D. Write a sentence for the word.**

I like _____

_____ .

© Newmark Learning, LLC

**47**

# little

Name _____

## Read

**A.  Read the word.**

little

How many sounds do you hear? Point to each box as you say the sounds. The gray box is silent.

| l | i | tt | l | e |

## Spell

**B.  Spell the word out loud as you write it.**

____ ____ ♡ ♡ ____ ♡

## Write

**C.  Write the word two times.**

_____   _____

**D.  Write a sentence for the word.**

_____

The _____

_____

_____ is little.

**48**

# look

Name _____

## Read

**A. Read the word.**

look

How many sounds do you hear?
Point to each box as you say the sounds.

| l | oo | k |

## Spell

**B. Spell the word out loud as you write it.**

_____  _____  _____  _____

## Write

**C. Write the word two times.**

_____   _____

**D. Write a sentence for the word.**

Look at the _____

_____

_____ .

© Newmark Learning, LLC

**49**

# make

## Read

**A. Read the word.**

make

How many sounds do you hear? Point to each box as you say the sounds. The gray box is silent.

m    a    k    e

## Spell

**B. Spell the word out loud as you write it.**

_____  _____  _____  ♡

## Write

**C. Write the word two times.**

_____    _____

**D. Write a sentence for the word.**

I can make a

_____

_____ .

50

# many

## Read

**A.  Read the word.**

many

How many sounds do you hear?

Point to each box as you say the sounds.

| m | a | n | y |

## Spell

**B.  Spell the word out loud as you write it.**

_____  ♡  _____  _____

## Write

**C.  Write the word two times.**

_____    _____

**D.  Write a sentence for the word.**

Many kids like to _____

_____ .

# me

## Read

**A.  Read the word.**

me

How many sounds do you hear?

Point to each box as you say the sounds.

m    e

## Spell

**B.  Spell the word out loud as you write it.**

_____    _____

## Write

**C.  Write the word two times.**

_____    _____

**D.  Write a sentence for the word.**

Is the _____

_____ for me?

# more

## Read

**A.** **Read the word.**

more

How many sounds do you hear? Point to each box as you say the sounds. The gray box is silent.

m    o    r    e

## Spell

**B.** **Spell the word out loud as you write it.**

____ ♡ ♡ ♡

## Write

**C.** **Write the word two times.**

_____    _____

**D.** **Write a sentence for the word.**

I want more _____

_____ .

# my

## Read

**A. Read the word.**

| my |

How many sounds do you hear?

Point to each box as you say the sounds.

| m | y |

## Spell

**B. Spell the word out loud as you write it.**

_____   _____

## Write

**C. Write the word two times.**

_____   _____

**D. Write a sentence for the word.**

My friend is _____

_____

_____ .

# new

## Read

**A. Read the word.**

new

How many sounds do you hear?

Point to each box as you say the sounds.

n    ew

## Spell

**B. Spell the word out loud as you write it.**

_____    _____    _____

## Write

**C. Write the word two times.**

_____    _____

**D. Write a sentence for the word.**

I have a new _____

_____ .

Name _____

## Read

**A. Read the word.**

no

How many sounds do you hear?

Point to each box as you say the sounds.

n     o

## Spell

**B. Spell the word out loud as you write it.**

_____ _____

## Write

**C. Write the word two times.**

_____    _____
- - - - - - - - - - - - - - - -    - - - - - - - - - - - - - - - -
_____    _____

**D. Write a sentence for the word.**

_____
- - - - - - - - - - - - - - - - - - - - - - - - - - - - - -
I have no
_____
- - - - - - - - - - - - - - - - - - - - - - - - - - - - - -
_____ .

# not

Name _____

## Read

**A.  Read the word.**

not

How many sounds do you hear?

Point to each box as you say the sounds.

n      o      t

## Spell

**B.  Spell the word out loud as you write it.**

_____   _____   _____

## Write

**C.  Write the word two times.**

_____   _____

**D.  Write a sentence for the word.**

I am not _____

_____

_____ !

© Newmark Learning, LLC

**57**

# of

## Read

**A. Read the word.**

of

How many sounds do you hear?

Point to each box as you say the sounds.

o    f

## Spell

**B. Spell the word out loud as you write it.**

## Write

**C. Write the word two times.**

_____    _____

**D. Write a sentence for the word.**

I see lots of _____

_____

_____ .

# off

## Read

**A.** **Read the word.**

off

How many sounds do you hear?

Point to each box as you say the sounds.

o | ff

## Spell

**B.** **Spell the word out loud as you write it.**

## Write

**C.** **Write the word two times.**

_____  _____

**D.** **Write a sentence for the word.**

Turn off the _____

_____ .

# old

## Read

**A.  Read the word.**

old

How many sounds do you hear?

Point to each box as you say the sounds.

o     l     d

## Spell

**B.  Spell the word out loud as you write it.**

 _____ _____

## Write

**C.  Write the word two times.**

_____  _____

**D.  Write a sentence for the word.**

I am _____

_____ years old.

Name _____

## Read

A. **Read the word.**

on

How many sounds do you hear?

Point to each box as you say the sounds.

o    n

## Spell

B. **Spell the word out loud as you write it.**

_____  _____

## Write

C. **Write the word two times.**

_____  _____

D. **Write a sentence for the word.**

The _____ is on the

_____ .

# one

Name _____

## Read

**A.  Read the word.**

one

How many sounds do you hear? Point to each box as you say the sounds. The gray box is silent.

| o | n | e |

## Spell

**B.  Spell the word out loud as you write it.**

## Write

**C.  Write the word two times.**

_____     _____

_____     _____

**D.  Write a sentence for the word.**

I see one _____

_____

_____ .

62

Name _____

## Read

**A. Read the word.**

| or |

How many sounds do you hear?

Point to each box as you say the sounds.

| o | r |

## Spell

**B. Spell the word out loud as you write it.**

_____   _____

## Write

**C. Write the word two times.**

_____   _____

**D. Write a sentence for the word.**

Do you like _____ or

_____ ?

Name _____

## Read

**A. Read the word.**

other

How many sounds do you hear?

Point to each box as you say the sounds.

o | th | e | r

## Spell

**B. Spell the word out loud as you write it.**

♡ _____ _____ _____ _____

## Write

**C. Write the word two times.**

_____  _____

**D. Write a sentence for the word.**

The other kids can _____

_____

_____ .

Name _____

**Read**

A.  **Read the word.**

our

How many sounds do you hear?

Point to each box as you say the sounds.

| ou | r |

**Spell**

B.  **Spell the word out loud as you write it.**

_____  _____  _____

**Write**

C.  **Write the word two times.**

_____    _____

D.  **Write a sentence for the word.**

Our school is _____

_____

_____ .

Name _____

## Read

**A.   Read the word.**

out

How many sounds do you hear?

Point to each box as you say the sounds.

ou     t

## Spell

**B.   Spell the word out loud as you write it.**

_____   _____   _____

## Write

**C.   Write the word two times.**

_____   _____

**D.   Write a sentence for the word.**

We ran out of _____

_____ .

# people

Name _____

## Read

**A.** **Read the word.**

people

How many sounds do you hear? Point to each box as you say the sounds. The gray box is silent.

| p | eo | p | l | e |

## Spell

**B.** **Spell the word out loud as you write it.**

## Write

**C.** **Write the word two times.**

_____    _____

**D.** **Write a sentence for the word.**

Some people _____

_____ .

# play

## Read

**A.  Read the word.**

play

How many sounds do you hear?

Point to each box as you say the sounds.

p | l | ay

## Spell

**B.  Spell the word out loud as you write it.**

_____  _____  _____  _____

## Write

**C.  Write the word two times.**

**D.  Write a sentence for the word.**

I like to play _____

_____ .

# pull

Name _____

**A.   Read the word.**

pull

How many sounds do you hear?

Point to each box as you say the sounds.

| p | u | ll |

**Spell**

**B.   Spell the word out loud as you write it.**

_____ ♡ ♡ ♡

**Write**

**C.   Write the word two times.**

_____   _____

**D.   Write a sentence for the word.**

Can you pull the _____

_____ ?

Name _____

## Read

**A.  Read the word.**

put

How many sounds do you hear?

Point to each box as you say the sounds.

p     u     t

## Spell

**B.  Spell the word out loud as you write it.**

_____  ♡  _____

## Write

**C.  Write the word two times.**

_____     _____

**D.  Write a sentence for the word.**

Put that _____

_____

_____ .

# read

## Read

**A.** Read the word.

read

How many sounds do you hear?

Point to each box as you say the sounds.

| r | ea | d |
|---|----|---|

## Spell

**B.** Spell the word out loud as you write it.

_____ _____ _____ _____

## Write

**C.** Write the word two times.

_____     _____

**D.** Write a sentence for the word.

I like to read _____

_____

_____ .

Name _____

## Read

**A.** **Read the word.**

run

How many sounds do you hear?

Point to each box as you say the sounds.

r    u    n

## Spell

**B.** **Spell the word out loud as you write it.**

_____ _____ _____

## Write

**C.** **Write the word two times.**

_____     _____

**D.** **Write a sentence for the word.**

Can you run to the _____

_____ ?

72

# said

Name _____

## Read

**A.  Read the word.**

said

How many sounds do you hear?

Point to each box as you say the sounds.

| s | ai | d |

## Spell

**B.  Spell the word out loud as you write it.**

## Write

**C.  Write the word two times.**

_____    _____

**D.  Write a sentence for the word.**

She said _____

_____

_____ .

# see

## Read

**A.  Read the word.**

see

How many sounds do you hear?

Point to each box as you say the sounds.

| s | ee |
|---|----|

## Spell

**B.  Spell the word out loud as you write it.**

_____   _____   _____

## Write

**C.  Write the word two times.**

_____   _____

**D.  Write a sentence for the word.**

I can see _____

_____ .

# she

## Read

**A. Read the word.**

she

How many sounds do you hear?

Point to each box as you say the sounds.

sh | e

## Spell

**B. Spell the word out loud as you write it.**

_____   _____   _____

## Write

**C. Write the word two times.**

_____   _____

**D. Write a sentence for the word.**

She is _____

_____ .

Name _____

## Read

**A. Read the word.**

| some |

How many sounds do you hear? Point to each box as you say the sounds. The gray box is silent.

| s | o | m | e |

## Spell

**B. Spell the word out loud as you write it.**

## Write

**C. Write the word two times.**

_____    _____
- - - - - - - - - - - - -    - - - - - - - - - - - - -

**D. Write a sentence for the word.**

Some dogs _____

_____

_____ .

# ten

## Read

**A. Read the word.**

ten

How many sounds do you hear?

Point to each box as you say the sounds.

t    e    n

## Spell

**B. Spell the word out loud as you write it.**

_____  _____  _____

## Write

**C. Write the word two times.**

_____    _____

**D. Write a sentence for the word.**

Ten men can _____

_____ .

# that

## Read

**A. Read the word.**

that

How many sounds do you hear?

Point to each box as you say the sounds.

th     a     t

## Spell

**B. Spell the word out loud as you write it.**

_____  _____  _____  _____

## Write

**C. Write the word two times.**

_____     _____

**D. Write a sentence for the word.**

That is a _____

_____ .

# the

## Read

**A.  Read the word.**

the

How many sounds do you hear?

Point to each box as you say the sounds.

th    e

## Spell

**B.  Spell the word out loud as you write it.**

## Write

**C.  Write the word two times.**

_____    _____

**D.  Write a sentence for the word.**

The _____ is

_____ .

# their

## Read

**A. Read the word.**

their

How many sounds do you hear?

Point to each box as you say the sounds.

| th | ei | r |

## Spell

**B. Spell the word out loud as you write it.**

_____  _____

## Write

**C. Write the word two times.**

_____  _____

_____  _____

**D. Write a sentence for the word.**

Their school is _____

_____

_____ .

# them

## Read

**A. Read the word.**

them

How many sounds do you hear?

Point to each box as you say the sounds.

th    e    m

## Spell

**B. Spell the word out loud as you write it.**

_____ _____ _____ _____

## Write

**C. Write the word two times.**

_____    _____

**D. Write a sentence for the word.**

Tell them to _____

_____

_____ .

# then

Name _____

## Read

**A. Read the word.**

then

How many sounds do you hear?

Point to each box as you say the sounds.

| th | e | n |

## Spell

**B. Spell the word out loud as you write it.**

_____  _____  _____  _____

## Write

**C. Write the word two times.**

_____  _____

**D. Write a sentence for the word.**

Then I _____

_____ .

82

© Newmark Learning, LLC

# there

## Read

**A. Read the word.**

there

How many sounds do you hear? Point to each box as you say the sounds. The gray box is silent.

| th | e | r | e |

## Spell

**B. Spell the word out loud as you write it.**

_____ _____  ♡ ♡ ♡

## Write

**C. Write the word two times.**

_____  _____

**D. Write a sentence for the word.**

There is my _____

_____

_____ .

# these

Name _____

## A. Read the word.

these

How many sounds do you hear? Point to each box as you say the sounds. The gray box is silent.

| th | e | s | e |

## Spell

## B. Spell the word out loud as you write it.

_____ _____ _____

## Write

## C. Write the word two times.

_____     _____

_____     _____

## D. Write a sentence for the word.

These books are _____

_____ .

# they

## Read

**A.   Read the word.**

they

How many sounds do you hear?

Point to each box as you say the sounds.

th    ey

## Spell

**B.   Spell the word out loud as you write it.**

_____ _____ ♡ ♡

## Write

**C.   Write the word two times.**

_____    _____

**D.   Write a sentence for the word.**

They are _____

_____

_____ .

# this

Name _____

**Read**

**A.   Read the word.**

this

How many sounds do you hear?
Point to each box as you say the sounds.

th    i    s

**Spell**

**B.   Spell the word out loud as you write it.**

_____  _____  _____  _____

**Write**

**C.   Write the word two times.**

_____    _____

**D.   Write a sentence for the word.**

This is a _____

_____

_____  .

**86**

© Newmark Learning, LLC

Name _____

## Read

**A. Read the word.**

three

How many sounds do you hear?

Point to each box as you say the sounds.

| th | r | ee |

## Spell

**B. Spell the word out loud as you write it.**

_____ _____ _____ _____ _____

## Write

**C. Write the word two times.**

_____     _____

**D. Write a sentence for the word.**

Three kids went _____

_____ .

Name _____

## Read

**A.  Read the word.**

to

How many sounds do you hear?

Point to each box as you say the sounds.

t     o

## Spell

**B.  Spell the word out loud as you write it.**

## Write

**C.  Write the word two times.**

_____     _____

**D.  Write a sentence for the word.**

We go to _____

_____ .

Name _____

## Read

**A. Read the word.**

two

How many sounds do you hear? Point to each box as you say the sounds. The gray box is silent.

| t | w | o |

## Spell

**B. Spell the word out loud as you write it.**

## Write

**C. Write the word two times.**

_____    _____
_____    _____

**D. Write a sentence for the word.**

I see two _____

_____ .

Name _____

## Read

**A. Read the word.**

up

How many sounds do you hear?

Point to each box as you say the sounds.

u    p

## Spell

**B. Spell the word out loud as you write it.**

_____   _____

## Write

**C. Write the word two times.**

_____   _____

**D. Write a sentence for the word.**

The _____

_____ is up.

Name _____

## Read

**A. Read the word.**

use

How many sounds do you hear? Point to each box as you say the sounds. The gray box is silent.

| u | s | e |

## Spell

**B. Spell the word out loud as you write it.**

## Write

**C. Write the word two times.**

_____    _____

**D. Write a sentence for the word.**

Use the _____ to _____ .

# want

Name _____

**A.  Read the word.**

want

How many sounds do you hear?

Point to each box as you say the sounds.

| w | a | n | t |

**Spell**

**B.  Spell the word out loud as you write it.**

____  ♡  ____  ____

**Write**

**C.  Write the word two times.**

_____    _____

**D.  Write a sentence for the word.**

I want to _____

_____

_____ .

92

# was

## Read

**A.** **Read the word.**

was

How many sounds do you hear?

Point to each box as you say the sounds.

| w | a | s |

## Spell

**B.** **Spell the word out loud as you write it.**

## Write

**C.** **Write the word two times.**

_____   _____

**D.** **Write a sentence for the word.**

I was _____

_____ .

# we

## Read

**A. Read the word.**

we

How many sounds do you hear?

Point to each box as you say the sounds.

w    e

## Spell

**B. Spell the word out loud as you write it.**

_____   _____

## Write

**C. Write the word two times.**

_____    _____

**D. Write a sentence for the word.**

We can _____

_____ .

# were

## Read

**A. Read the word.**

were

How many sounds do you hear? Point to each box as you say the sounds. The gray box is silent.

| w | e | r | e |
|---|---|---|---|

## Spell

**B. Spell the word out loud as you write it.**

____ ♡ ♡ ♡

## Write

**C. Write the word two times.**

_____    _____

**D. Write a sentence for the word.**

We were not _____

_____ .

# what

## Read

**A.** **Read the word.**

what

How many sounds do you hear?

Point to each box as you say the sounds.

wh    a    t

## Spell

**B.** **Spell the word out loud as you write it.**

_____ _____ ♡ _____

## Write

**C.** **Write the word two times.**

_____    _____

**D.** **Write a sentence for the word.**

What is _____

_____

_____ ?

**96**

# when

## Read

**A.** **Read the word.**

when

How many sounds do you hear?

Point to each box as you say the sounds.

wh    e    n

## Spell

**B.** **Spell the word out loud as you write it.**

_____  _____  _____  _____

## Write

**C.** **Write the word two times.**

_____    _____

**D.** **Write a sentence for the word.**

When will _____

_____

_____ ?

# where

Name _____

**A. Read the word.**

where

How many sounds do you hear? Point to each box as you say the sounds. The gray box is silent.

wh · e · r · e

## Spell

**B. Spell the word out loud as you write it.**

_____ _____

## Write

**C. Write the word two times.**

_____    _____

**D. Write a sentence for the word.**

Where is _____

_____ ?

# which

## Read

**A.** **Read the word.**

which

How many sounds do you hear?

Point to each box as you say the sounds.

| wh | i | ch |

## Spell

**B.** **Spell the word out loud as you write it.**

_____  _____  _____  _____  _____

## Write

**C.** **Write the word two times.**

_____    _____

**D.** **Write a sentence for the word.**

Which book _____

_____ ?

Name _____

## Read

**A.  Read the word.**

who

How many sounds do you hear?

Point to each box as you say the sounds.

wh    o

## Spell

**B.  Spell the word out loud as you write it.**

## Write

**C.  Write the word two times.**

_____    _____

**D.  Write a sentence for the word.**

Who will _____

_____ ?

# why

## Read

**A. Read the word.**

why

How many sounds do you hear?

Point to each box as you say the sounds.

wh | y

## Spell

**B. Spell the word out loud as you write it.**

_____  _____  _____

## Write

**C. Write the word two times.**

_____    _____
- - - - - - - - - - - - - -    - - - - - - - - - - - - - -

**D. Write a sentence for the word.**

- - - - - - - - - - - - - - - - - - - - - - - - - - - - - - - - - - -

Why is _____

_____

- - - - - - - - - - - - - - - - - - - - - - - - - - - - - - - - - ?

# will

## Read

**A.** **Read the word.**

will

How many sounds do you hear?

Point to each box as you say the sounds.

w    i    ll

## Spell

**B.** **Spell the word out loud as you write it.**

## Write

**C.** **Write the word two times.**

_____    _____

**D.** **Write a sentence for the word.**

I will _____

_____

_____ .

**102**

# with

Name _____

## Read

**A. Read the word.**

with

How many sounds do you hear?

Point to each box as you say the sounds.

w    i    th

## Spell

**B. Spell the word out loud as you write it.**

_____  _____  _____  _____

## Write

**C. Write the word two times.**

_____    _____

**D. Write a sentence for the word.**

Go with me to _____

_____ .

© Newmark Learning, LLC

**103**

# write

Name _____

## Read

**A. Read the word.**

write

How many sounds do you hear? Point to each box as you say the sounds. The gray boxes are silent.

| w | r | i | t | e |

## Spell

**B. Spell the word out loud as you write it.**

♡ ____ ____ ____ ♡

## Write

**C. Write the word two times.**

_____  _____

**D. Write a sentence for the word.**

I like to write _____

_____ .

© Newmark Learning, LLC

# yes

## Read

**A.   Read the word.**

yes

How many sounds do you hear?

Point to each box as you say the sounds.

| y | e | s |

## Spell

**B.   Spell the word out loud as you write it.**

_____   _____   _____

## Write

**C.   Write the word two times.**

_____   _____

_____   _____

**D.   Write a sentence for the word.**

Yes I can _____

_____

_____ !

# you

## Read

**A. Read the word.**

you

How many sounds do you hear?

Point to each box as you say the sounds.

y    ou

## Spell

**B. Spell the word out loud as you write it.**

____ ♡ ♡

## Write

**C. Write the word two times.**

_____    _____

**D. Write a sentence for the word.**

Are you _____

_____ ?

**106**

# your

## Read

**A. Read the word.**

your

How many sounds do you hear?

Point to each box as you say the sounds.

| y | ou | r |

## Spell

**B. Spell the word out loud as you write it.**

____ ♡ ♡ ♡

## Write

**C. Write the word two times.**

_____    _____

**D. Write a sentence for the word.**

Your school is _____

_____ .

# Fluency Phrases

Practice reading these phrases.

Write your own phrase for each high-frequency word.

| Read It | Write It |
| --- | --- |
| **A** cat | |
| **All** of us | |
| I **am** happy | |
| Cats **and** dogs | |
| We **are** | |
| **At** the park | |
| **Be** my friend | |
| A **big** dog | |
| **Can** we go | |
| **Come** with me | |
| I **could** | |
| **Did** you | |
| It is **different** | |

# Fluency Phrases

Practice reading these phrases.

Write your own phrase for each high-frequency word.

| Read It | Write It |
|---|---|
| I **do** | |
| **Down** the hill | |
| We **eat** | |
| **Eight** legs | |
| It is **for** me | |
| **Four** fun books | |
| I am **from** here | |
| **Give** it to me | |
| **Go** there | |
| It is **good** | |
| I **had** it | |
| He **has** | |
| We **have** | |

# Fluency Phrases

Practice reading these phrases.
Write your own phrase for each high-frequency word.

| Read It | Write It |
| --- | --- |
| **He** is a friend | |
| **Her** book | |
| **Here** it is | |
| Tell **him** | |
| **His** book | |
| **How** can I | |
| **I** can | |
| **In** the box | |
| It **is** big | |
| **It** is little | |
| **Jump** up | |
| I **know** it | |
| Please **let** me | |

# Fluency Phrases

Practice reading these phrases.

Write your own phrase for each high-frequency word.

| Read It | Write It |
| --- | --- |
| I **like** it | |
| The **little** bug | |
| **Look** at me | |
| I can **make** it | |
| **Many** friends | |
| Tell **me** | |
| **More** of that | |
| **My** friend | |
| A **new** book | |
| I have **no** time | |
| **Not** for me | |
| A lot **of** | |
| Turn it **off** | |

# Fluency Phrases

Practice reading these phrases.

Write your own phrase for each high-frequency word.

| Read It | Write It |
|---|---|
| The **old** man | |
| **On** the table | |
| **One** time | |
| Dogs **or** cats | |
| **Other** kids | |
| **Our** favorite food | |
| **Out** of time | |
| Some **people** | |
| **Play** with me | |
| **Pull** it down | |
| **Put** it there | |
| **Read** that book | |
| **Run** in the park | |

# Fluency Phrases

Practice reading these phrases.
Write your own phrase for each high-frequency word.

| Read It | Write It |
|---|---|
| She **said** yes | |
| I **see** | |
| **She** can | |
| **Some** kids | |
| **Ten** little men | |
| **That** is good | |
| **The** book | |
| **Their** school | |
| Please help **them** | |
| **Then** I said | |
| **There** it is | |
| **These** books | |
| **They** can | |

# Fluency Phrases

Keep going!

Practice reading these phrases.
Write your own phrase for each high-frequency word.

| Read It | Write It |
| --- | --- |
| **This** is good | |
| **Three** kids | |
| **To** the school | |
| **Two** legs | |
| **Up** in the sky | |
| **Use** it | |
| I **want** | |
| I **was** not | |
| **We** can | |
| We **were** | |
| **What** is it | |
| **When** is it | |
| **Where** is it | |

# Fluency Phrases

Practice reading these phrases.

Write your own phrase for each high-frequency word.

| Read It | Write It |
| --- | --- |
| **Which** one | |
| **Who** can | |
| **Why** am I | |
| We **will** | |
| Come **with** me | |
| I can **write** | |
| **Yes** I can | |
| **You** are happy | |
| It is **your** book | |

# Let's Assess

Listen to your child or student read each word aloud.

Put a check mark under "Accurate" if the word is read correctly.

Put another check mark under "Automatic" if the word is read fast.

| Word | Accurate | Automatic |
|------|----------|-----------|
| 1. a | | |
| 2. I | | |
| 3. the | | |
| 4. on | | |
| 5. can | | |
| 6. big | | |
| 7. am | | |
| 8. go | | |
| 9. at | | |
| 10. he | | |
| 11. is | | |
| 12. like | | |
| 13. my | | |
| 14. did | | |
| 15. play | | |
| 16. run | | |
| 17. and | | |
| 18. had | | |
| 19. see | | |
| 20. ten | | |
| 21. in | | |
| 22. up | | |
| 23. yes | | |
| 24. has | | |
| 25. you | | |

| Word | Accurate | Automatic |
|------|----------|-----------|
| 26. it | | |
| 27. him | | |
| 28. let | | |
| 29. little | | |
| 30. no | | |
| 31. said | | |
| 32. will | | |
| 33. to | | |
| 34. be | | |
| 35. his | | |
| 36. what | | |
| 37. give | | |
| 38. one | | |
| 39. me | | |
| 40. read | | |
| 41. use | | |
| 42. where | | |
| 43. look | | |
| 44. this | | |
| 45. she | | |
| 46. not | | |
| 47. some | | |
| 48. that | | |
| 49. have | | |
| 50. down | | |

| Word | Accurate | Automatic |
|------|----------|-----------|
| 51. are | | |
| 52. come | | |
| 53. for | | |
| 54. do | | |
| 55. good | | |
| 56. from | | |
| 57. here | | |
| 58. jump | | |
| 59. make | | |
| 60. or | | |
| 61. how | | |
| 62. out | | |
| 63. put | | |
| 64. more | | |
| 65. them | | |
| 66. two | | |
| 67. we | | |
| 68. there | | |
| 69. when | | |
| 70. your | | |
| 71. why | | |
| 72. they | | |
| 73. was | | |
| 74. our | | |
| 75. with | | |

| Word | Accurate | Automatic |
|------|----------|-----------|
| 76. could | | |
| 77. eat | | |
| 78. all | | |
| 79. her | | |
| 80. of | | |
| 81. write | | |
| 82. three | | |
| 83. were | | |
| 84. four | | |
| 85. pull | | |
| 86. then | | |
| 87. want | | |
| 88. these | | |
| 89. which | | |
| 90. old | | |
| 91. who | | |
| 92. their | | |
| 93. people | | |
| 94. other | | |
| 95. off | | |
| 96. new | | |
| 97. many | | |
| 98. know | | |
| 99. different | | |
| 100. eight | | |

**You did great! Now color me to celebrate!**

118